D1092968

Global Warming:
Apocalypse Or Hot Air?

Roger Bate
Director, IEA Environment Unit

Julian Morris
Research Fellow, IEA Environment Unit

with a Foreword by

Wilfred Beckerman
Emeritus Fellow, Balliol College, Oxford

Published by the
IEA Environment Unit

1994

First Published in March 1994

Second Impression August 1994

by

THE ENVIRONMENT UNIT
INSTITUTE OF ECONOMIC AFFAIRS
2 Lord North Street, Westminster,
London SW1P 3LB

Studies on the Environment No. 1

All Rights Reserved

ISBN 0-255 36331-1

Set in Plantin and Univers

Printed in Great Britain by
Goron Pro-Print Co Ltd, Lancing, W. Sussex

Table of Contents

Foreword .... *Wilfred Beckerman* 5

The Authors... 8

Acknowledgements.. 8

Introduction 9

1. An Outline of the Science of Global Warming.. 11

   The Greenhouse Effect 11

   The Enhanced Greenhouse Effect 13

   A Brief History of Climate Modelling 15

   Climate Data.. 18

   How Do the Models Perform? 20

   Data Problems.. 21

   Alternative Explanations of Climate Change 23

   Climate Change Impacts of Increased CO_2 25

   Conclusion 26

2. The Economics of Global Warming 28

   Economic Analysis..................................... 28

   Measuring Costs and Benefits............................ 31

   Problems With Long-run Forecasting 33

   Uncertainty 35

   Free Lunches... 39

   Conclusion 41

3. Policy Issues 43

    Limiting Fossil Fuel Use 43

    Subsidising Energy Efficiency Improvements........... 46

    Research into the Social and Economic Costs of
       Global Warming.. 47

    Research into Climatology..................................... 47

    Research into Geoengineering 47

    A 'What If?' Scenario 48

Conclusion.. 49

Questions for Discussion 50

Glossary.. 51

Further Reading... 52

List of Figures

    Figure 1: Relative Greenhouse Warming
       Potential of Emissions... 12

    Figure 2: Global Average Temperature Anomalies
       1890-1990, based on Reference Period 1950-79 ... 19

    Figure 3: Comparison of Satellite and Land-
       based Data, 1979-90.. 24

List of Tables

    Table 1: Model forecast temperature increase
       for a doubling of CO_2 (°C)................................. 18

    Table 2: Comparison of studies estimating changes in
       world GDP over a period, given restrictions placed
       on CO_2 emissions... 36

Foreword

The public is constantly warned that the pollution generated by economic activity constitutes a real threat to the survival of the human race. In particular, we are told, unless drastic action is taken to curtail carbon emissions from the burning of fossil fuels, climate change will take place that will have calamitous effects on standards of living in the course of the next century. At the slightest sign that governments do not mean to press ahead with vigorous policies to reduce carbon emissions, cohorts of eco-doomsters rush to warn us that we are living on the edge of the abyss, that urgent action is needed to save the planet, that even if serious global warming is not certain it is quite likely and would be irreversible, so that – in the name of some so-called 'precautionary principle' – immediate action must be taken to avert the threat of catastrophic climate change.

In view of the nature and amount of media coverage given to such visions of global catastrophe, it is not surprising that most members of the public are taken in by it all. As a result time, energy and financial resources that could have been devoted to dealing with the innumerable serious environmental problems facing the world in both rich and poor countries are diverted to dealing with those that are more glamorous, but far less important.

Of course, these are more exciting and telegenic than issues such as how to moderate pollution of underwater aquifers from agricultural activities, or how to dispose of industrial waste or household garbage, or how to help developing countries improve their access to safe drinking water or sanitation (the lack of which kills several million children every year), or how to estimate the severity of the threat to bio-diversity and its significance. Apocalyptic warnings that the world will come to an end unless we mend our wicked ways, cut our standard of living, give up our aspirations for increased prosperity, and so on, have been the essence of evangelical crusades throughout the ages. The preachers move us by their compassion for future generations, by their ability to see through the sham of modern consumerism, and by the strength of their moral fibre and their aesthetic sensitivities to the true beauties of life. It is to the credit of the public's social conscience that, under the mistaken impression that the apocalyptic predictions are true, it is ready to dig into its pockets to finance the organisations that help disseminate the alarming message.

More important, the support that such messages arouse amongst the public means that they have some influence on the stance of almost all political parties. In turn this has a harmful impact on policies. Old-fashioned evangelical crusaders, who merely told us that all our woes were the result of inherent human wickedness, never did any harm and may even have done some good. In the first place, they were basically right. (They might have indicated stupidity as well, but one can understand their reluctance to do so.) And, in the second place, there was not much that governments could do to change human nature.

But today's environmental crusaders who tell us that we must impose heavy restrictions on the use of fossil fuels would, if taken seriously, impose enormous unjustified costs on society, and probably on those sections of society that can least bear them. And, unfortunately, governments feel pressurised by the force of public opinion to take action along these lines, both alone and in conjunction with other nations.

An alternative course of action would be to expose the shoddiness of the apocalyptic predictions. Unfortunately, governments cannot be expected to undertake this task. Hence it is left to private individuals and institutions to

6

try to breach the barriers to the dissemination of good news and the media's natural preference for reporting only the disasters.

This IEA study is one such attempt. The authors set out, first, the many limitations on the so-called scientific 'consensus' over global warming. They then show that such economic analysis as has been made by no means supports the view that climate change would impose intolerable burdens on future generations. The authors of this study have done so in simple terms that are easily accessible to any interested person who wants to hear the other side of the debate.

Climate change is a scientific problem of mind-boggling complexity. Nobody can claim that we are near conclusive answers. But nobody should be panicked into hasty action on the basis of very one-sided accounts of what the answers are. If this study does no more than bring home to the public the fact that there is another side to the argument and that it is time for a more balanced public debate over the whole issue of environmental catastrophe, it will take its place amongst the long list of important IEA publications that have successfully challenged prevailing orthodoxies.

February 1994   WILFRED BECKERMAN
                    Emeritus Fellow, Balliol College, Oxford

Global Warming: Apocalypse or Hot Air? is the first publication of the new IEA Environment Unit. A new unit is appropriate because environmental issues are now so prominent and because so many activities are regulated in the name of environmental protection. The views expressed are those of the authors, not of the Institute (which has no corporate view), its Trustees, Advisers or Directors.

C.R.

The Authors

Roger Bate is Director of the Environment Unit at the Institute of Economic Affairs and a regular columnist in the IEA's journal *Economic Affairs*. He is reading for a PhD at Cambridge University and lectures part-time on environmental economics. He is a fellow of the Royal Society of Arts.

He has a BA in Economics from Thames Valley University and an MSc in Environmental and Resource Economics from University College, London. He was supported by the Charles G. Koch Charitable Foundation as an Environmental Research Associate at the Competitive Enterprise Institute, Washington DC, which published his paper 'Pick a Number: A Critique of the Contingent Valuation Methodology and its Application in Public Policy' (1994).

Julian Morris has an MA in Economics from the University of Edinburgh and an MSc in Environmental and Resource Economics from University College, London. He has worked as an econometrician for Commerzbank in Frankfurt and is currently Environmental Research Fellow at the IEA.

Acknowledgements

We would like to thank John Blundell for having the vision to create the Environment Unit and for supporting us throughout, and Lorraine Mooney for reading many early drafts. We also thank the three anonymous referees who commented on a draft of this Paper.

Roger Bate also thanks the Earhart Foundation of Ann Arbor, Michigan, for generous funding of his work.

R.B.

J.M.

8

Introduction

According to whom you trust, 'global warming' will either destroy the world's agriculture or enrich it; will cause the seas to rise as ice melts, or the seas to fall as ice forms; it will cause summers to be unbearably hot, or merely lead to mild winters.

Of course, the irony is that only a few years ago models of weather patterns – the basis of most global warming models – were so poor that people would laugh openly at forecasts of the next day's thunderstorms or heatwaves. In 1987, for example, the Met Office failed to foresee, even 12 hours ahead, the severity of the most devastating storm to hit Britain for a hundred years.

Given the very large uncertainties involved in making forecasts (a problem familiar to most economists), we should be sceptical of any theory about the future of the world which purports to be fact. In particular, we should be especially sceptical of people who believe it is necessary to exaggerate their claims in order to convince us of the validity of their story. Such is the case with Dr Stephen Schneider, global warming protagonist and adviser to US Vice-President Albert Gore Jr. In October 1989 Schneider gave an interview to *Discover* magazine, in which he said:

> 'To capture the public's imagination ... we have to offer up some scary scenarios, make simplified, dramatic statements, and little mention of any doubts one might have. ... Each of us has to decide the right balance between being effective and being honest. I hope that means being both.'[1]

Such admissions make the claims of the protagonists questionable, especially in the absence of corroborative

---

1 *Discover Magazine*, October 1989.

evidence. A 1991 poll of the members of the American Meteorological Society found that,

> 'Among those actively involved in research [into climatology] and publishing frequently in peer reviewed journals, 0% believe any warming has occurred so far.'[2]

Despite this lack of empirical support, the 'international community' has deemed international action appropriate. Following the Rio Summit of June 1992, government officials decided to limit greenhouse gas emissions to 1990 levels by the year 2000.[3]

In this Paper, we wish to present the evidence for and against the various theories which seek to explain the variations in climate over time; to explain why one theory – the impact of increases of trace atmospheric gases – has come to dominate the debate; to discuss how economists have contributed to the debate; and to suggest how policy-makers should respond.

---

2 R. S. Lindzen, 'Global Warming: The Origin and Nature of Alleged Scientific Consensus', OPEC seminar on the environment, Vienna, 13-15 April 1992. Richard Lindzen has been Sloan Professor of Meteorology at MIT since 1983.

3 The history of this regulation follows a familiar pattern. Environmental pressure groups have for some years been promoting the *apocalyptic vision*; so successful have these agents of doom been that by the late 1980s the UN had been persuaded to commission a report on the scientific evidence for climate change – the Intergovernmental Panel on Climate Change (IPCC) report. The scientific journal *Nature* ran an important editorial (15/11/90) on the dismissive attitude of IPCC officials towards non-mainstream views. They said: 'IPCC's failure to discuss dissenting opinions, perhaps even to dismiss them, was a mistake...there are many recent illustrations of how received opinion proved to be mistaken.' The UN subsequently convened the Conference on Environment and Development (UNCED) in Rio in June 1992. At UNCED many governments, clearly persuaded by the political consequences of taking no action and perhaps seeing the possibilities for tax revenue and bureaucratic control, signed the Framework Convention on Climate Change (UNFCCC).

1. An Outline of the Science of Global Warming

The Greenhouse Effect

The temperature of interstellar space is approximately -250°C, whereas the average surface temperature of the earth is 15°C. This difference, of 265°C, is primarily due to the sun's radiation. However, 20°C is attributable to some of the earth's atmospheric gases[4] – which bring about the 'greenhouse effect'.[5] Without this effect the average surface temperature of the earth would be -5°C and it would be uninhabitable.

Greenhouse Gases (GHGs), such as CO_2 and water vapour,[6] are transparent to short wavelength radiation (e.g. sunlight), but opaque to longer wavelength radiation (e.g. infra-red emitted by the earth). These gases, therefore, let sunlight through to warm the earth but trap

---

[4] Nitrogen and oxygen, which comprise 99% of the atmosphere, play no part in the greenhouse effect.

[5] Snow, ice, clouds or water vapour and other 'white bodies' reflect a great deal of incoming short-wave radiation back into space (the 'albedo effect'). Hence, penetrating solar radiation is calculated to be reduced by 30% from that of a comparative 'black body' planet. Some climatologists have claimed that because of this albedo effect the greenhouse warming is 33°C, not 20°C. They argue that if there were no greenhouse gases (GHGs) one could calculate the difference as 33°C. However, by assuming no GHGs one also removes all reflective clouds, snow and ice, the albedo is therefore less, and more radiation would reach the earth. The fundamental point is that these climatologists are overestimating the power of GHGs to warm the planet and therefore give these gases greater warming potential than they warrant.

[6] Other GHGs of importance are: nitrous oxide (N_2O), methane (CH_4), chlorofluorocarbons (CFCs). The first two GHGs occur naturally and have existed for billions of years, whereas CFCs were not present in the atmosphere before human intervention. N_2O comes from fossil fuel and biomass burning; CH_4 comes from fossil fuels, rice paddies and the stomachs of ruminants such as cattle, sheep and termites; CFCs come from refrigerants, aerosol propellants and industrial solvents. For more detail on the GHGs see R. Balling, *The Heated Debate: Greenhouse Predictions vs Climate Reality*, San Francisco: Pacific Research Institute, 1992.

11

**Figure 1: Relative Greenhouse Warming
Potential of Emissions**

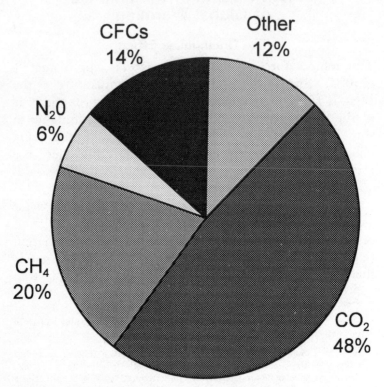

Source: P. Michaels, *op. cit.*,p.13, citing the Environmental
Protection Agency.

infra-red radiation from the earth and warm the planet by
20°C.

Each of these gases has a different GHG 'potential' –
each traps a different amount of radiation per molecule.
To make a comparison of the GHG contribution of each
gas possible, the relative contribution compared to CO_2 is
calculated. While all other anthropogenic (human
produced) GHGs have higher GHG potentials than CO_2,
their atmospheric concentrations are low so their overall
contribution is less. Figure 1 shows the relative

greenhouse warming potential of anthropogenic[7] emissions.[8]

The term 'greenhouse effect' is something of a misnomer: while CO_2 and water vapour, in common with glass, are efficient at retaining outgoing long-wave radiation, true greenhouses retain heat primarily by preventing convection.

The Enhanced Greenhouse Effect

In 1986, on network television, Senator Albert Gore Jr. (now Vice-President of the United States) said that 'there is no longer any significant disagreement in the scientific community that the greenhouse effect is real'. However, as Professor Michaels points out, this

'is about as profound as a revelation that all scientists now agree that the earth is round. The implication and the connection that most people make are that all scientists agree that global temperatures are rising disastrously as a result of the enhancement of the greenhouse effect. That conclusion is simply wrong.'[9]

The enhanced greenhouse effect (also popularly called 'global warming') is a theory, first described by Svente

---

7 Water vapour 'accounts for nearly 70% of the overall radiative effect' (Balling, *op. cit.*, p.17) but it is not included in Figure 1 as man's activities do not alter its concentration.

8 As Dr John Emsley (chemist at Imperial College, University of London) points out: 'CO_2 is close to its saturation point and hence the role of CO_2 in any warming will decline [relatively] over time.' ('The Global Warming Trial', BBC Radio Four, 16 September 1993.) Steven Schneider explained this process thus: 'the addition of more CO_2 does not substantially increase the infra-red opacity of the atmosphere ... because the 15 micron CO_2 band ... "saturates".' (*Science*, 1971). To clarify: gases only absorb radiation at specific frequencies (those which match the frequency at which the molecules 'resonate'). Once all the radiation at these specific frequencies has been absorbed the addition of more gas will not increase the overall amount of absorption – and these frequencies are described as 'saturated' (analogously to, for example, brine when no more salt will dissolve in it).

9 Patrick Michaels, *Sound and Fury: The Science and Politics of Global Warming*, Washington DC: Cato Institute, 1992, p.9. Patrick Michaels is Climatologist for the Commonwealth of Virginia and is associated with the Cato Institute.

Arrhenius[10] in 1896, which explains how the additions of GHGs, through human activity, will trap more infra-red radiation and consequently may lead to an increase in atmospheric temperatures.

The greenhouse effect is considered to be fact, whereas the enhanced greenhouse effect is an unproven theory. There has never been a scientific consensus (although there is a popular consensus today) that man's activities have been warming the earth. Indeed, since Arrhenius there seems to have been little mention of the enhanced greenhouse effect until the 1950s when, probably due to some hot summers, it became fashionable again.[11]

The 1960s and 1970s were significantly cooler than the 1950s and global warming theory lost ground to ice-age theory. Global cooling had many adherents, as global warming has today, and again man was to blame. It was claimed that dust, as a by-product of industrial activity, was reflecting too much sunlight away from the earth's surface and cooling the planet.[12] Books such as *Ice* by Sir Fred Hoyle, *The Cooling* by Lowell Ponte and *The Genesis Strategy* by Stephen Schneider sold millions of copies.

The present furore over global warming really started in 1988. In June of that year the head of NASA's Goddard Space Institute, James Hansen, testified before the US Senate that 'global warming is now sufficiently large that we can ascribe with a high degree of confidence a cause and effect relationship to the greenhouse effect'.[13]

The press, ever eager for apocalyptic predictions, ran stories on looming disasters and picked up Hansen's

10 S. Arrhenius, 'On the influence of carbonic acid in the air upon the temperature of the ground', *Philosophical Magazine*, Vol. 41, 1896, pp.237-76.

11 The person most responsible was the late Professor of Ocean Sciences, Roger Revelle, at the Scripps Institute of Oceanography, University of California, La Jolla, CA, USA.

12 See Schneider's comments in note 8.

13 Testimony before the Senate Committee on Energy and Natural Resources, 23 June 1988.

prediction that 1988 would be the warmest year on record. Perhaps unsurprisingly, he was wrong, but the damage had been done.

A Brief History of Climate Modelling

All climate models attempt to explain broad changes in climate. The modeller's knowledge of atmospheric chemistry and physics is then used to simulate changes in climate from some induced shock, such as a doubling of carbon dioxide.

Point Earth – Zero-Dimensional Models

Arrhenius modelled climate changes as though the earth were a point, simply analysing the net flows of radiation. He knew that GHGs reduced outflows of radiation and estimated that a doubling of CO_2 would lead to a 5°C increase in temperature, while a 50% increase in CO_2 would lead to a 3°C increase in temperature. Other models of this type produced similar results for a CO_2 doubling: Plass (3·6°C)[14], Moller (1·5°C).[15]

Despite his simplistic model, Arrhenius knew that the regional impacts of temperature change would be crucial. If the increase occurs in winter, at night and at high latitudes, as Arrhenius himself suggested, might this not actually increase crop yields? As Professor Michaels explains:

> '[W]hat matters is *how* the climate changes. The "how" question includes matters of timing, seasonality, spatial distribution of changes, and even whether or not changes are equally distributed between day and night.'[16]

---

14 G. Plass, 'The CO_2 theory of climate change', *Tellus*, No.8, 1956, pp.140-53.

15 F. Moller, 'On the influence of changes in the CO_2 concentration in air on the radiation balance of the earth's surface and on the climate', *Journal of Geophysical Research*, Vol. 68, 1963, pp. 3,877-86.

16 P. Michaels, *op. cit.*, p. 31.

Line Earth – One-Dimensional Models

These models were the first attempts to get close to answering the 'how' question. They extend the 'point earth' in a line to the top of the atmosphere, a series of points at different places in the atmosphere forming a vertical line. They include more atmospheric physics than the point, using basic cloud physics and convective processes.

> 'The influence of various gases could be carefully specified in such a radiative-convective model. [This model] … is surprisingly well suited to the greenhouse problem.'[17]

However, these models predicted similar temperature rises, of around 4°C, from a doubling of CO_2.[18]

Flat Earth – Three-Dimensional Models

(a) Land-atmosphere models

These encompass the vertical line earth-atmosphere models, as above, whilst also detailing the latitudinal and longitudinal components of the planet. They are usually designed in $500Km^2$ grids which, although crude, mean that many thousands of grids are required to represent the earth. With the vertical component stretching up many kilometres, there are over 20,000 boxes representing the globe. These models are extremely complex, taking months of super-computer time to predict a decade of change, and in principle should monitor climate more accurately than those in only one dimension.

---

17 R. Balling, *op. cit.*, p. 35.

18 S. Manabe & R. Wetherald, 'The effects of doubling the CO_2 concentration on the climate of a general circulatory model', *Journal of the Atmospheric Sciences*, Vol. 32, 1975, pp. 3-15.

(b)   Land-atmosphere-ocean models

More advanced models (often one of the land-atmosphere models updated) attempt to add ocean-atmosphere inter-actions, as well as land-atmosphere activity.

Both (a) and (b) above are called General Circulatory Models (GCMs) because they attempt to model all the wind patterns of the earth. They also include differential equations designed to

> 'simulate changes in atmospheric pressure ... [net flows of radiation] ... thermal patterns, wind vectors, moisture levels, precipitation, clouds, ice and snow, and on and on ... These models ... are tremendous achievements in computing, applied mathematics, and atmospheric physics'.[19]

However, even the most up-to-date GCMs are 'extremely primitive'[20] and, as Michaels points out, GCMs

> 'were designed as teaching and research tools for advanced study of the atmosphere. They were not originally intended to "forecast" the future, and most principled investigators spend much more time talking about the limitations of GCMs than they do touting their predictions'.[21]

These models predict increases in temperature, for a doubling of CO_2, similar to the predictions of the simpler models, of between 1·9°C and 5·2°C. The advanced GCMs are so complex that whole teams of scientists are required to design and run them. They tend therefore to be known by the names of institutions rather than by those of individual scientists. The predictions of the major models are listed in Table 1.

---

[19] R. Balling, *op. cit.*, p. 36.

[20] R. Lindzen, 'The Global Warming Trial', BBC Radio Four, 16 September 1993.

[21] P. Michaels, *op. cit.*, p. 32.

Table 1
Model forecast temperature increase
for a doubling of CO_2 (°C)

Model	°C
UK Met. Office (UKMO)	1.9 – 5.2
Oregon State University (OSU)	2·8 – 4·4
Goddard Institute for Space Studies (NASA)	3·9 – 4·8
Geophysical Fluid Dynamics Laboratory (GFDL)	2·0 – 4·0

Source: Intergovernmental Panel on Climate Change, *IPCC Scientific Assessment*, Cambridge: CUP, 1990, pp. 69-91.

Climate Data

Greenhouse Gases (GHGs)

There are few certainties in climatology. However, it seems that two features have been accepted as fact. The first, as pointed out above, is that the 'greenhouse effect' is real, the second is that man's activities over the last two centuries have led to an increase of between a quarter and a third of atmospheric CO_2. Similar increases of other GHGs have occurred:

> 'Equivalent CO_2 levels [total increase in all GHG warming potential] were approximately 290 ppm [parts per million] at the beginning of the Industrial Revolution; by 1900, the equivalent CO_2 had risen to about 310 ppm... [T]he best estimate of equivalent CO_2 for 1990 is over 430 ppm – since the beginning of the Industrial Revolution, we have increased the equivalent CO_2 by approximately 50%.'[22]

These data are not contested by any reputable source.

Temperature

The surface temperature of the planet has varied greatly over the past one thousand years. In AD 1200 extensive

---

[22] R. Balling, *op. cit.*, p. 32.

Figure 2: Global Average Temperature Anomalies 1890-1990, based on Reference Period 1950-79

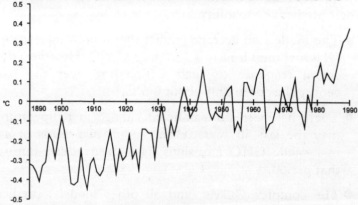

Source: *Trends '91*, Oak Ridge, Tennessee: CDIAC, 1991.

vineyards were found in southern England, and the average temperature was 2°C higher than today. By 1600 Britain was in the midst of the little ice-age when 'frost fairs' were held on the River Thames and the average temperature was about 1°C lower than today. More recently, Dickens wrote of the cold winters of the 19th century.

The measurement of temperature this century has been far more widespread and detailed than ever before. As Figure 2 shows, world temperature has fluctuated widely, on average increasing about 0·5°C[23] over the first half century, but changing less since 1940.[24]

---

[23] No one global average temperature is calculated due to the difficulty of comparing temperature recordings at different sites. Not all sites are at the same altitude and not all samples are taken at the same time of day. By 'appropriate weighting' Jones & Wigley arrive at an average figure of sorts. They take a reference period (1950-79) against which anomalies in temperature are measured. They chose the 1950-79 period as fairly stable. Why they take a reference period at all is not explained. However, one impact of the re-basing is to make the temperature rise in the 1980s more dramatic.

[24] P. Jones & T. Wigley, 'Global Warming Trends', *Scientific American*, Vol. 263, 1990, pp. 84-91, cited in T. Boden, R. Sepanski & F. Stoss (eds.), *Trends 91: A compendium of data on global change*, Oak Ridge, Tennessee: Carbon Dioxide Information Analysis Center, 1991.

How Do the Models Perform?

Ex-post testing of the models has exposed serious flaws in their predictive capability.

- The models on average predict that a 50% increase in GHGs should lead to a warming of 2°C. However, the actual response to such a doubling over the last century has been only about 0·5°C.[25]

- There has been no significant change in temperature over the last 50 years, even though two-thirds of all man-made GHG emissions have been added during that period.[26]

- The complex GCMs (and all other models) predict that higher latitudes should warm more than equatorial regions. However, as has been noted by the two climatologists who developed the temperature record used as the basis for the IPCC report:

  'There has really been no warming in the polar regions at all, even though this is where the computer models predict warming should be greatest.'[27]

- The models primarily analyse radiation effects, essentially ignoring the other two methods of heat transference – convection and conduction. For example, in 1991 the UK Meteorological Office's climate model was still predicting the same rainfall level for Ireland and the Sahara Desert.

- To make the models fit existing data, modellers have made assumptions about atmospheric physics that are known to be false. For example, one model had clouds reflecting only 90% of the solar radiation that they

---

25 There is considerable debate over the validity of the data sets used by some researchers: see below, p. 21.

26 P. Michaels, *op. cit.*

27 P. Jones & T. Wigley, *op. cit.*, p.91.

actually reflect. Professor Michaels estimates that the consequence of this

> 'is roughly equivalent to moving the earth about two million miles closer to the sun ... The lowering [of the clouds' reflective quality] was necessary because the computer simulated the pre-greenhouse-enhancement climate at around 5°C colder than the present temperature. ... the same as at the height of the last ice age.'[28]

Another problem is that because GCMs have trouble simulating the current climate, let alone the projected carbon dioxide increase, modellers have resorted to trying to eliminate the real world from their predictions. They simulate the earth as best they can, then double the concentration of CO_2 and see what the temperature difference is. As Professor Lindzen explains:

> 'models are largely verified by comparison with other models. Given that models are known to agree more with each other than with nature ... this approach does not seem promising.'[29]

Data Problems

If the data do not fit the models, then there are inaccuracies in either the data or the models, or both. Which is true?

Temperature variations depend on season and on latitude far more than on gas concentration, so it is difficult to find a good average temperature measurement for the planet. It seems likely that 0·5°C (the figure generally cited) is not representative of the global temperature increase over the past century. One problem, highlighted by Balling, is that although most of the planet is water, most of the temperature sensors are located on land, and worse still, in urban areas.

---

28 P. Michaels, *op. cit.*, p.32.
29 R. Lindzen, *op. cit.*, p. 4.

Urban Warming?

Concrete, asphalt, bricks and mortar hold heat better than trees and grass; less convection occurs in towns; and large towns, with numerous cars, often have low-level ozone which acts to produce a mini greenhouse effect, trapping heat locally. In general, urban areas are warmer than the surrounding countryside. Indeed, large cities such as London can be a couple of degrees warmer than the home counties (the 'Urban Heat Island Effect'). A study by Ferguson and Clarke[30] showed that even small US towns with populations in the hundreds had measurable urban heat effects. For example, Realitos (a Texan town of 240 people) had a winter urban-rural differential of +0·4°C.

Realising this problem, Balling and Idso[31] selected 961 rural measurement stations (discarding over 5,000 urban ones) in the USA to measure temperature over the period 1920-1990. They found a cooling of 0·15°C.

> 'We have to be careful when we look at people who say they have detected global warming because what they may have detected is URBAN warming'. [32]

Updates

Recent developments in satellite sensing have made possible temperature measurements not subject to heat islands. In a NASA study[33] microwave emissions from oxygen molecules in the lower atmosphere were measured, allowing the determination of their temperature to

---

30 Ferguson & Clarke, mimeo, National Oceanic and Atmospheric Administration, 1984.

31 R. Balling & S. Idso, 'Historical Temperature Trends in the United States and the Effect of Urban Population Growth', *Journal of Geophysical Research*, No. 94, 1992, pp. 3,359-63.

32 *Ibid.*, p.3,360.

33 R. Spencer & J. Christy, 'Precise Monitoring of Global Temperature Trends From Satellite', *Science*, Vol. 247, 1990, p.1,558; also 'Precision and Radiosonde validation of Satellite Grid Point Temperature Anomalies', *Journal of Climate*, August 1992.

an accuracy of 0·01°C. From 1979 to 1990 there was no change in temperature. Recent updates, to 1994, still show no warming.[34] When confronted with this type of data (even accepting that this time-period is short) the response by ardent global warming advocates is typified by Dr Stephen Schneider:

> '[L]looking at every bump and wiggle of the record is a waste of time... So, I don't set very much store in looking at the direct evidence'.[35]

Dr Chris Folland of the UK Meteorological Office (UKMO), and a contributor to the IPCC Policy-makers summary, went even further, saying:

> '[T]he data don't matter... Besides we [the UN] are not basing our recommendations [for immediate reductions in CO_2 emissions] upon the data; we're basing them upon the climate models.'[36]

No global study we could locate has distinguished rural sites. Therefore, it is impossible to say what warming (if any) there has been this century. However, the data seem to be upwardly biased, so it is likely that the average temperature increase is less than 0·5°C. This makes the models' average prediction of 2°C even less likely.

Figure 3 compares the results of the NASA study, which recorded no change in temperature, with the data shown in Figure 2 – the most commonly cited data source – over the same period (1979-90).

Alternative Explanations of Climate Change

Temperature changes of up to 0·5°C over 100 years are well within the expected (cyclical) range of natural

---

[34] J. R. Christy & R. T. McNiden, *Nature*, Vol. 367, 1994, p. 325.

[35] Interview for 'The Greenhouse Conspiracy', UK: Channel 4 Television, August 1990.

[36] C. Folland, Presentation at Asheville, North Carolina, reported in P. Michaels, *op. cit.*, pp. 82-3.

Figure 3: Comparison of Satellite and Land-based Data, 1979-90

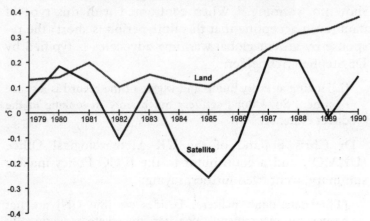

Source: CDIAC, *Trends '91*, Oak Ridge,
Tennessee: CDIAC, 1991.

variability. Several competing explanations of this natural fluctuation have been proposed.

Solar Activity

As Figure 2 shows, there have been short cycles of warming and cooling over the past century. A study in November 1991 by Friis-Christensen and Lassen[37] found a correlation between solar cycle length[38] and global temperature of 0·95,[39] significantly higher than that found for temperature and GHG concentration, which 'suggests that the sun and not the greenhouse effect has been the

---

37 E. Friis-Christensen & K. Lassen, 'Length of the Solar Cycle: An Indicator of Solar Activity Closely Associated with Climate', *Science*, Vol. 254, 1 November 1991, pp. 698-700.

38 It is in fact an inverse relationship. The shorter the cycle, it is alleged, the higher the level of radiation and hence temperature.

39 Correlation measures how closely the changes in two sets of data are related. A figure of 1 indicates that the relationship is 'perfect' and 0 indicates that there is no apparent relationship between the changes in each data set. 0.95 is therefore indicative of a very strong relationship.

controlling factor in climate changes over the last 100 years'.[40]

Other possible explanations of temperature variations abound, too lengthy for this publication, but probably the most cogent is the role of aerosol sulphates put forward by Balling:[41]

> '[S]ulfur compounds injected into the stratosphere by large volcanic eruptions certainly act to cool the earth by scattering incoming solar radiation.'[42]

Climate Change Impacts of Increased CO_2

Although the impact of CO_2 as a warming gas is near its limit, due to the wavelength saturation explained above (note 8, p.13), the effects of increased CO_2 on plant life are worth noting.

CO_2 is not a pollutant: it is a gas vital for our survival. With water and light, CO_2 is the third key nutrient for photosynthesis in plants. However, the concentration of CO_2 is often so low as to reduce photosynthetic activity. It is the 'limiting nutrient'. Indeed, some plants die at concentrations of CO_2 below 100 ppm. Professor Idso's experiments[43] indicate that increases in CO_2 lead to greater plant bulk and improved foliage – an obvious advantage for farmers – but, perhaps more staggering still, plants require less water under such conditions. This means that plants can grow in drier conditions, perhaps even improving the growing potential of marginal land such as the Sahel region of Africa.[44]

---

[40] R. Jastrow, *Global Warming Update*, Washington DC: George C. Marshall Institute, July 1992, p. 19.

[41] R. Balling, *op. cit.*, pp. 119-31.

[42] *Ibid.*, p. 121.

[43] K. Idso, *Plant Responses To Rising Levels Of Atmospheric Carbon Dioxide*, Tempe, Arizona: Institute For Biospheric Research, 1992.

[44] 'In terms of plant responses to atmospheric CO_2 enrichment ... 93% ... are positive ... [T]he mean growth enhancement for a 300 ppm rise in CO_2 of the air is 52%. For a 600 ppm rise it is 69%.' (K. Idso, *op. cit.*)

As Professor Lindzen said recently:[45] '[N]ature usually has negative feedbacks, it would be poor engineering ... to have positive feedbacks as the models suggest.' Increasing CO_2 leads to increased photosynthetic activity which limits the growth rate of CO_2 in the atmosphere. Robert Jastrow emphasised Lindzen's point when discussing clouds and the possibility of global warming:

'The greenhouse heating may lead to the formation of more clouds, shielding the earth's surface and cooling the planet... The increase in cloud cover would be a negative feedback.'[46]

Furthermore, a well-established fear of global warming is that ice caps will melt causing sea levels to rise, and drowning whole islands. However, this hypothesis is not supported by evidence from recent satellite observations, which suggest that Antarctic ice caps grew during the warm years of the 1980s, nor by visual observations of glaciers such as Norway's Eventyrisen, which has also grown. The growth of ice caps during warm years increases the albedo effect, another negative feedback, thereby mitigating any warming.

Conclusion

On balance the evidence suggests that:

- The greenhouse effect, which clearly exists, has the effect of maintaining a comfortable planetary temperature.

- GHG concentrations have approximately doubled since the Industrial Revolution. CO_2, the most important anthropogenic GHG, is approaching its warming limit due to wavelength saturation.

- There has been a measured increase in the average global surface temperature of approximately 0.5°C

---

45 R. Lindzen, comments to the audience at the 'Global Warming Trial', *op. cit.*
46 R. Jastrow, *op. cit.*, p. 28.

over the last century. A 0·5°C change is within natural variability. This measured increase is, however, likely to be attributable largely to urban warming and hence actual global warming may be very slight.

- The enhanced greenhouse effect (or 'global warming') is a highly debatable theory which does not correlate well with the empirical data.

- The models used to predict global warming, although very complex, do not include all possible, or even important, variables. Their ex-post predictions are not borne out when empirically tested.

- Temperature is more highly correlated with solar cycle length over the last century than with changes in GHG concentration.

- The effects of increased CO_2 are likely to be beneficial as they include increased crop yields and reduced water requirements of plants.

- The effects of warming, if it occurs, are not clearly established. If warming occurs at night, in winter and at high latitudes, as is predicted, then the effects may on balance be beneficial. However, there is too much uncertainty to predict whether a positive or negative result will occur.

- The overall effects of GHG emissions are unknown but are unlikely to be seriously good or seriously bad, because the global ecosystem appears to be 'engineered' for stability. Negative feedbacks seem to be the norm. For example, increases in temperature tend to increase precipitation which increases cloud cover and hence reduces temperature. The negative feedbacks in place mean that a 'climate apocalypse' (either through warming or ice-age) is unlikely to occur in the foreseeable future.

2. The Economics of Global Warming

Section 1 considered the empirical evidence for and against the scientific hypothesis that anthropogenic emissions of GHGs are causing and are expected to cause significant warming of the earth's atmosphere. It concluded that the evidence for such a causal effect is minimal.

In this section we consider the evidence for and against claims made by economists and other social scientists that the possibility of global warming, however slight, necessitates the imposition of restrictions on emissions of GHGs.

Economic Analysis

Since the end of the 1980s, governments across the (developed) world have been spending huge sums of tax-payers' money funding research into ostensibly economic aspects of the 'global warming problem'.[47] Most of these research studies conclude that GHG emissions should be limited even though, given the scientific uncertainty concerning the impact of anthropogenic GHGs on the global climate, it seems premature to be making any such pronouncements. In the words of Professor William Nordhaus:

'We now move from the *terra infirma* of climate change to the

---

[47] In fact the literature dates back at least to the late 1970s: see, for example, W. D. Nordhaus, *Strategies for the Control of Carbon Dioxide*, Cowles Foundation Discussion Paper No. 443, 1977; and W. D. Nordhaus, 'Economic Growth and Climate – the Carbon Dioxide Problem', *American Economic Review*, Vol. 67, No. 1, 1977, pp. 341-46. But, like so many 'public' policies, funding became available on a huge scale only after the pressure groups had become sufficiently vocal.

terra incognita of the social and economic impacts of climate change.'[48]

Three main types of analysis have been employed.

(i)   Cost-Benefit Analysis (CBA)

CBA is an attempt to quantify all the *aggregate* costs and benefits of a policy. Some of the more significant problems with such analysis are as follows:

- To measure *aggregate* costs and benefits we must first know the *individual* costs and benefits.[49] Since we can neither observe nor predict the impacts of a policy on individuals, such aggregate evaluation is impossible.

- One consequence of ignoring the effects of a policy on individuals, as Cost-Benefit analysts in fact do, is that policies based on such CBAs will inevitably result in gains to some (frequently identifiable) persons at the cost of other (rarely identifiable) persons. This kind of arbitrary redistribution is clearly undesirable.

- CBA requires information not only about the preferences of living individuals but also those of all individuals who will ever be affected by the policy. Such information is clearly not available.

- Even those who believe we can accurately estimate the impacts of a policy on all concerned must still decide how to weight individual preferences. Central to this debate has been the question of how one might appropriately discount the future. Since discount rates vary across individuals it is not surprising that a single

---

[48] W.D. Nordhaus, 'To Slow Or Not To Slow: The Economics of The Greenhouse Effect', *Economic Journal*, Vol. 101, 1991, pp.920-37.

[49] An *aggregate* measure is clearly the sum of *individual* measures – to assert otherwise is illogical.

aggregrate 'social discount rate' has proven elusive[50] – it is not estimable.

(ii) Cost Analysis

It has been suggested that since policy-makers seem intent on regulating emissions of GHGs, one ought to ask what the cost of such policies might be. It is true that the costs of alternative policies might be estimated, but such estimates cannot justify the policies themselves. For example, if there is insufficient scientific evidence of a threat from global warming to justify an abatement policy, identifying a 'low cost' abatement policy is irrelevant.

The main problem with such cost analysis is, as we shall show, that estimates are based on forecasts of a highly uncertain future.

(iii) Game Theory

Economics, in the guise of game theory, has attempted to assess the likelihood of achieving international co-operation to abate GHG emissions. These studies (usually dependent on CBA) are universally pessimistic about the possibility of co-operation over a GHG treaty (because, even assuming that the climate apocalyptics are correct, the benefits of co-operation are not much higher than the costs). The implication is that even if agreement is reached in principle, it is unlikely to be stable and has little chance of ratification because some party is always likely to have an incentive to renege.[51]

---

50 Scott, for example, estimated the social rate of discount to be between 1 and 10.5 per cent per annum (M. Scott, 'The Test Rate of Discount and Changes in Base-Level Income in the United Kingdom', *Economic Journal*, June 1977) – a range rather too broad to be of any practical use.

51 Space does not permit a fuller discussion of these issues here, but see, for example, R. F. Kosobud & T.A. Daly, 'Global Conflict or Cooperation over the CO_2 Climate Impact?', *Kyklos*, No. 37, pp. 638-59; S. Barrett, *Convention on Climate Change: Economic Aspects of Negotiations*, Paris: OECD, 1992; and S. Barrett, *Self-Enforcing International Environmental Agreements*, London: London Business School, mimeo, August 1992.

Measuring Costs and Benefits

While we believe that the arguments noted above against the use of CBA are overwhelming, there are further problems which relate to the specific measurement techniques employed. Since these techniques constitute the bulk of economic research funded by taxpayers' money, we shall give a more detailed critique of their use.

In order to measure the costs and benefits of a policy which will have impacts on economic activity for many years, it is clearly necessary to be able to forecast those impacts. Many teams of economists have developed forecasting models for precisely this purpose. Like climate models, all economic forecasting models 'are nothing but a series of interacting differential equations'.[52] However, this oversimplifies the situation, because there are certain differences in modelling strategy. It is consequently worth briefly describing the four main model types.

Model Taxonomy

1. *Disaggregated Partial Equilibrium Models* use forecasts of certain 'exogenous' variables, typically fuel prices and population growth,[53] to determine the baseline level of energy use. An energy-GDP function then determines the actual level of GDP.[54]

The predictive validity of such models depends on both the accuracy of the forecasts of the exogenous variables and the validity of the specification of the price function. We are unaware of any tests of either the *ex-post* or *ex-ante* validity of this functional specification.

---

[52] P. Michaels, *op. cit.*, p. 82.

[53] Prices are typically assumed to follow a logistic function, and population a trend. In the real world, of course, neither population nor energy price is truly exogenous.

[54] The prime example of this type of specification is the International Energy Authority/Oak Ridge Associated Universities model developed by Edmonds & Reilly and used by many global warming researchers. See J. Edmonds & J.M. Reilly, 'A long-run global energy-economic model of carbon dioxide release from fossil fuel use', *Energy Economics*, Vol. 5(2), 1983, pp.74-88.

2. *Partial Equilibrium Growth Models* typically take GDP and technological change as 'exogenous' variables, and use an aggregate production function (usually of a Constant Elasticity of Substitution or CES form) to determine overall economic output.

The problems with such a specification are similar to those for the disaggregated form, although in this case the model specification has been shown to be a poor representation of the 'real' world (*ex-post*): Boero *et al.* note that CES production functions 'have failed nearly every econometric test they have faced.'[55]

Both types of partial equilibrium models are typically used to estimate the costs of implementing policies to control GHG emissions by raising the price of fossil fuels.[56]

3. *Optimal Control Models* go a step further than the growth models by including environmental feedbacks: typically they seek to maximise global consumption (or some function thereof) over some period (typically 100 years), subject to various economic and environmental constraints. They suffer from the same problems as growth models, but are often further biased by the inclusion of spurious environmental impacts.

4. *General Equilibrium (GE) Models*[57] differ from the above model types in that all the parameters assigned to variables[58] (economic and environmental) are en-

---

55 G. Boero, R. Clarke and L.A. Winters, *The Macroeconomic Consequences of Controlling Greenhouse Gases: A Survey*, London: HMSO, 1991.

56 Another problem is that two of the key parameters (see note 58) of each model, the elasticities of substitution between fuels and between factors of production, have both proven to be extremely difficult to estimate.

57 Also called 'Computerised' General Equilibrium (CGE) models. This may be an attempt to make them sound more sophisticated. In fact, all the models described need to be calibrated and simulated using computers: to do so by hand would take decades (but the results would be just as poor).

58 A parameter is the numerical constant indicating the relationship between two variables within a model.

dogenously determined. Such a specification gives the impression of a truer picture of the world economy, but suffers even more severely from parameter instability[59] and is subject to the same criticism as optimal control models with regard to the environmental variables.[60]

One other model 'type' is frequently identified in the literature – the Input-Output or Bottom-Up model, a very basic form of Disaggregated Partial Equilibrium model, which extrapolates current energy-use patterns. As Boero *et al.* have noted, 'by their very nature [they] cannot plot the effects of simultaneous substitutions in all sectors and countries on factor prices'.[61] Unless we have good reason to believe that the underlying parameters are extremely stable (which we do not), such models are unreliable forecasting tools.

Problems With Long-run Forecasting

Economics, unlike the natural sciences, relies for its data on the unpredictable actions of human beings. Economic forecasts are an attempt to predict aggregate economic activity – the collective economic behaviour of all individuals considered. While trends in economic activity may be observed *ex-post*, it is dangerous to suppose that these trends will continue – individual behaviour is likely to change, both as a result of autonomous decisions and in reaction to external events. Predicting changes in

---

[59] Because all parameters are simultaneously determined, small errors in any single parameter will be multiplied. Since human behaviour is unpredictable (see 'Problems with Long-run Forecasting', above), the 'true values' of these parameters are unlikely to be constant, so these errors will feed through to make forecasts extremely unreliable.

[60] Examples of such models are: J-M. Burniaux, J.P. Martin, G. Nicoletti and J.O. Martins, *The Costs of Policies to Reduce Global Emissions of CO_2: Initial Simulation Results with GREEN*, OECD, Dept. of Economics and Statistics Working Paper 103, June 1991; and J. Whalley & R. Wigle, 'The International Incidence of Carbon Taxes', in R. Dornbusch & J.M. Poterba (eds.), *Global Warming: Economic Policy Responses*, Cambridge, Mass.: MIT, 1991, pp.233-63.

[61] G. Boero *et al.*, *op. cit.*

trends, as many of the modellers attempt,[62] requires a certain degree of clairvoyance.

The main problem in attempting to forecast the economic environment of the latter part of the 21st century (which many environmental models do) is that we know neither the tastes of the future inhabitants of the planet nor the technologies which will be available to satisfy those tastes. Moreover, we cannot now know how the technologies of the 21st or 22nd centuries would deal with any climatic changes which might occur.[63] As Professor Thomas Schelling writes:

'Imagine it were 1900 and the climate changes associated with a three-degree average temperature increase were projected to 1992. On what kind of world would we superimpose either a vaguely described potential change in climate or even a specific description of changes in weather in all seasons of the year, even for our own country [the USA in this case]. There would have been no way to assess the impact of the changing climates on air travel, electronic communication, the construction of skyscrapers, or the value of California real estate. Most of us worked outdoors; life expectancy was 47 years (it is now 75); barely a fifth of us lived in cities of 50,000 or more. Anticipating the automobile, we might have been concerned with whether wetter and drier seasons would bring more or less mud, not anticipating that the nation's roads would be thoroughly paved. The assessment of the effects on health would be without antibiotics or inoculation. And in contrast to most contemporary concern with the popular image of hotter summers to come, I think we would have been more concerned about warmer winters, later frost in autumn and earlier thaw in spring.

---

62 Models frequently include parameters, such as the elasticity of substitution between factors of production, which are merely 'guessed'.

63 If (and it is a big if) any changes do occur, it seems likely that humanity would adapt (and at far less cost than by limiting GHG emissions): see the discussion later about 'geoengineering' (below, p. 47).

'If the world...is going to change as much in the next 90 years as it has changed in the 90 just past, we are going to be hard put to imagine the effects of climate changes.'[64]

Table 2 summarises the results of the main studies which have attempted to estimate the costs of restricting CO_2 emissions. These studies all chose different baseline emission reductions, thereby making direct comparison difficult. Nevertheless, there is considerable disagreement over the probable impact of policies. Most notably, Edmonds and Reilly[65] estimate that, allowing for a 162% *increase* in CO_2 above 1990 levels will reduce GDP by 5%; and Mintzer[66] estimates that a 67% *decrease* in CO_2 below 1990 levels will reduce world GDP by 3%.[67]

Uncertainty

Some economists have suggested that uncertainty concerning the probable impact of an increase in anthropogenic GHGs and, by implication, the attendant uncertainty surrounding estimates of the economic impact of policies, might not affect the type of policy chosen. The argument is succinctly put by Professor David Pearce:[68]

'From the economic standpoint, the uncertainty is unlikely to alter the appropriate policy stance, [as detirmined by CBA]

---

64 T. C. Schelling, 'Some Economics of Global Warming', *American Economic Review*, January 1992.

65 J. Edmonds & J.M. Reilly, 'A long-run global energy-economic model of carbon dioxide release from fossil fuel use', *Energy Economics* 5(2), 1983, pp.74-88.

66 I. Mintzer, *A Matter of Degrees: The Potential for Controlling the Greenhouse Effect*, Research Report No. 5, Washington DC:World Resources Institute, 1987.

67 In an attempt to overcome the uncertainty problem, several researchers have simulated their models using Monte-Carlo analysis. However, it is unclear whether this methodology actually improves matters, since uncertainty in the Knightian sense (as opposed to risk) cannot be represented probabilistically.

68 Professor Pearce is Director of the Centre for Social and Economic Research on the Global Environment (CSERGE – pronounced, apocalyptically, 'sea-surge').

Table 2
Comparison of studies estimating changes in world GDP over a period, given restrictions placed on CO_2 emissions

Study	Type of Model	Projection Period	Level of Emissions[1]	Change in World GDP[2]
Edmonds & Reilly (1990)	IEA/ORAU[3]	1975-2050	+162% (1990)	−5.0%
Mintzer (1987)	IEA/ORAU	1975-2075	−67% (1990)	−3.0%
Cline (1989)	IEA/ORAU	1975-2075	−31% (1990)	−7.4%
Edmonds & Barnes (1990)	IEA/ORAU	1975-2025	0% (1988)	−1.8%
Whalley & Wigle (1990)	GE[4]	1990-2030	−50% (2030)	−4.2%
Burniaux et al. (1991)	GREEN[5]	1990-2025	+17% (1985)	−1.8%[6]
Manne & Richels (1990)	Global 2100[7]	1990-2100	+16% (1990)	−5%
Nordhaus (1992)	DICE[8]	1990-2105	0% (1990)	−1.3%[9]

Notes to Table 2:

1 Reduction in level of CO_2 emissions from reference year (in brackets).

2 Change in world GDP by end year of the projection period.

3 A disaggregated partial equilibrium model, developed by Edmonds & Reilly.

4 A general equilibrium model developed by Whalley & Wigle.

5 A general equilibrium model developed by Burniaux et al.

6 In 2020.

7 A partial equilibrium growth model, based on Manne's ETA-MACRO model.

8 Optimal control model, incorporating a climate function based on a simple model developed by Stephen Schneider.

9 Assuming no deleterious effects from projected rise in GHG emissions.

Source: Adapted from Boero et al., *op. cit.*

provided certain conditions are met. These are:

(a) that if warming occurs it will impose significant damage;

(b) that the damage is irreversible;

(c) that the initial costs of controlling greenhouse gas emissions are low;

(d) that greenhouse gas controls bring incidental or joint benefits besides the containment of global warming.'[69]

However, these conditions are not met:

- We do not know how much damage (or improvement) will occur even if warming occurs – the uncertainty is so great that using standard statistical analysis one cannot reject the hypothesis that damage will be zero. So (a) does not hold.

- Since we do not know what kind of damage, if any, will occur we cannot say that this damage will be irreversible. So (b) does not hold.

In addition, if we accept the postulates of CBA, then, as Arrow and Fischer point out:

'Just because an action is irreversible does not mean that it should not be undertaken. Rather the effect of irreversibility is to reduce the benefits, which are then balanced against the costs in the usual way.'[70]

As Beckerman notes:

'If human beings took no action that would have irreversible consequences the human race would have ceased to exist long ago!'[71]

---

69 D. Pearce, 'The Role of Carbon Taxes in Adjusting to Global Warming', *Economic Journal*, Vol. 101, 1991, pp.938-48.

70 K. Arrow & A. Fischer, 'Environmental Preservation, Uncertainty and Irreversibility', *Quarterly Journal of Economics*, Vol. 88, 1974, pp. 312-19.

71 W. Beckerman, 'Global Warming: A Sceptical Economic Assessment', in D. Helm (ed.), *Economic Policy Towards the Environment*, Oxford: Blackwell, 1991, pp.52-85.

- Bearing in mind that demand for energy is inelastic with respect to price,[72] 'low' cost in (c), above, is not only subjective but also a *non sequitur*. As we shall see, the policies to which Pearce is referring – government subsidised energy conservation schemes and a carbon tax to restrict demand – would have to impose significant direct financial costs on individuals to be effective and would almost certainly further restrict their freedom. So (c) does not hold.

- The idea that one should limit emissions of GHGs on the grounds that they might be coincidental with the emission of some other supposed environmental hazard is disingenuous: if GHGs *of themselves* pose no threat, then it is surely more efficient (less costly) to limit emissions of these other substances independently.[73] So (d) does not hold.

While Pearce and others accept that the evidence in support of these conditions being met is contentious, it is claimed that uncertainty concerning future climate change is itself a reason to limit GHG emissions:

> '...even the central projections of global warming in the IPCC scenarios take the world into rates of warming, and, eventually, levels of warming outside the known tolerances of ecosystems in which mankind has a stake. If so, there is genuine uncertainty which alone should dictate a cautious stance in policy terms.'[74]

Such reasoning encourages two fallacies: firstly, that the IPCC policy-makers' summary is scientifically credible (which seems doubtful), and secondly, that policy should be based on fear of the unknown. Both propositions are

---

72 That is, a large increase (or decrease) in the price of energy will only result in a small decrease (or increase) in its consumption.

73 But we are not arguing that any emissions should be limited by government mandate, simply that Pearce's argument is inconsistent with CBA.

74 D. Pearce, *op. cit.*, p. 938.

extremely dangerous: the first discourages healthy scientific debate, whilst the second may lead to the enactment of extremely restrictive, expensive and wholly unnecessary policies.

Free Lunches

Some economists have argued that so-called 'no-regrets' policies should be enacted on the grounds that they confer 'social benefits' at no 'social cost', implying the proverbial free lunch.[75] When discussing this issue, most economists propose removing 'market imperfections', such as those said to exist in the markets for energy-efficient goods[76] and public transport,[77] by providing subsidies to these goods.

Energy Efficiency

Several arguments have been advanced to support the notion that the market for energy efficiency is imperfect. However, if it were truly economically efficient to install more energy-efficient equipment or insulation, then people would tend to do so. Examples of the arguments for intervention are:[78]

● The existence of information asymmetries: For example, information concerning the efficacy of energy efficiency improvements (and especially those already made to homes, factories, etc.) is not widely available. Since information providers of this kind already exist (at least in the US), one might suppose that their less

---

[75] Even W. D. Nordhaus, 'To Slow Or Not To Slow', *The Economist*, 7 July 1990, and W. Beckerman, *op. cit.*, recommend such no-regrets policies.

[76] For example, V. Brechling, D. Helm, and S. Smith, 'Domestic Energy Conservation: Environmental Objectives and Market Failures', in D. Helm (ed.), *Economic Policy Towards the Environment*, Oxford: Blackwell, 1991, pp.263-288.

[77] E. Symons, J. Proops & P. Gay, *Carbon Taxes, Consumer Demand and Carbon Dioxide Emission: A Simulation Analysis for the UK*, University of Keele, Department of Economics, 1991.

[78] See Brechling *et al.*, *op. cit.*

than widespread use is at least partly because the cost of acquiring this information (for instance, paying an inspector to survey property) exceeds the expected benefits. Perhaps if there were fewer regulations concerning the heat retention of buildings, such information providers might flourish (indeed, chartered surveyors might offer thermal efficiency surveys as an optional extra): at present, government inspectors probably crowd-out private providers.

- Non-appropriability of benefits: Installing insulation in tenanted housing, for example, benefits the occupant more than the owner, so owners have less incentive to install it. This is essentially the same problem as above, except it is perhaps more acute in that, while the price of the information is probably the same, the benefits (to short-term tenants at least) may be lower. The reply is, however, the same.

- Non-optimisation: Brechling *et al.* suggest that 'consumers may use inappropriate decision rules for weighing up costs and benefits in different time periods' and therefore do not buy as much energy efficiency as they would do under Brechling's decision rule. Unless there is some intrinsic reason why we should all become *Homo Brechlingus* we cannot see any reason for pursuing this point further.

Public Transport

With regard to 'public' transport, the real problem is not that it is inadequately funded by government, but that road and rail systems in most countries are not privately run, and are therefore not subject to the efficiency-inducing incentives of the market.[79]

---

79 See J. Hibbs, *On the Move...*, Hobart Paper 121, London: Institute of Economic Affairs, April 1993.

An Exception

However, there is one 'no-regrets' policy which does seem worth pursuing: remove all taxes and subsidies currently applied to fossil fuels. This is likely both to reduce GHG emissions and increase global economic output. Much of this efficiency gain would come from removing subsidies to coal. Such subsidies distort the market by reducing consumption of other, more efficient, sources of energy, while the tax revenues thereby spent crowd-out better investments.[80]

This policy is laudable because it gives agents greater freedom of choice and has the added bonus that such free agents are more efficient than governments at allocating resources.[81] However, such a policy would impose costs on some special interests who would be certain to oppose any such action.

Conclusion

● Uncertainty has been shown to play an important role in determining the costs and benefits of limiting GHG emissions, but this should make us more rather than less wary of imposing such limits. A high-risk investment is less attractive, all else being equal, than a low-risk investment.

---

[80] Two examples: First, China currently uses around four times more energy to produce a unit of GNP than any other nation (see A. S. Manne & R. G. Richels, 'Global CO_2 Emission Reductions – the Impacts of Rising Energy Costs', *The Energy Journal*, Vol. 12 (1), 1991, pp.87-107). This implies that in the long run China could quadruple its GNP without increasing its energy consumption. Secondly, the German state pays up to 10 times the world market price to produce coal in its state-supported industry. It is rather curious that the government officials of this country, whose inhabitants appear to have such high environmental ideals, wilfully squander tax revenues on subsidising the depletion of natural resources.

[81] See, for example, C. Robinson, *Energy Policy: Errors, Illusions and Market Realities*, IEA Occasional Paper No. 90, London: Institute of Economic Affairs, October 1993.

- Even assuming that the IPCC policy-makers' summary is a just interpretation of the science of global warming, forecasts of the costs and benefits of limiting GHG emissions suggest that under conditions of uncertainty we would do better not to impose any limits.[82]

- If the critics of the 'popular vision' are correct and there are no harmful effects from any build-up of GHGs over the next 100 years, then limiting emissions to 1990 levels for the whole period could reduce global output by significant amounts.

- So-called 'no-regrets' policies, with the exception of the elimination of government intervention in the energy market, have hidden costs: since the market is better at allocating resources than any central planner, such policies would create more distortions than are alleged to exist already.

- Free markets in energy will not only be efficient, but will also alert us to changes in environmental conditions – via the price mechanism – far faster than any model might do.[83]

[82] Making this assumption, W. D. Nordhaus (1992), *op. cit.*, estimates that the net benefits of an 'optimal' policy would be about 0·03% of total discounted world consumption from 1990 to 2105. Given the uncertainty surrounding such a forecast, and given the high probability of intervention failure, such a policy does not seem worthwhile.

[83] See, for example, F. L. Smith, 'Is Europe About to Commit Eco-Suicide? The Case Against Carbon Taxes', mimeo, Washington DC: Competitive Enterprise Institute.

3. Policy Issues

Section 1 discussed the scientific evidence (or, rather, the lack thereof) for global warming caused by anthropogenic GHG emissions. Section 2 reviewed the literature on the economics of the GHG problem. We now turn to the pressing issue of how policy-makers should respond to the call to take action given the evidence presented in the earlier sections.

There are five broad policy proposals currently being considered.

Limiting Fossil Fuel Use

The UN Framework Convention on Climate Change (UNFCCC) led to the signatories agreeing to limit CO_2 emissions to 1990 levels by the year 2000 (above, note 3, p.10). With the ostensible aim of meeting this target, governments and trading blocs have proposed imposing a tax on fossil fuels.[84] We believe that the UNFCCC is unnecessary and the policies proposed to meet the targets are inefficient.

It is unnecessary because:

1. The link between GHG emissions and global climatic change is not sufficiently well established, with the direction of any link as yet unknown. (The temperature and CO_2 record going back 150,000 years

---

[84] The precise form of tax is as yet undecided. Most economists talk about a 'Carbon Tax', which would mean that at some point in the chain from producer to consumer a levy (probably paid to the government of the state in which the sale takes place) is imposed on the sale of fossil fuels. The size of the tax would be proportional to the carbon content of the fuel (coal has the most, methane the least).

suggests that it is as likely that temperature changes determine CO_2 levels as the other way round.)[85]

2. Even if causality is shown at some time in the future, CO_2 appears to be close to its 'saturation' level, so further increases will have a diminishing impact on temperature. The implication is that we should be less concerned about CO_2 than the other GHGs (which in any case are believed to have only a marginal impact).

3. Increased CO_2 concentrations improve photosynthetic activity, thereby increasing crop yields which, in turn, reduce CO_2 levels. Higher CO_2 concentrations also lower plants' requirements for water and other nutrients, thereby increasing the fertility of arid areas such as the Sahel.

4. There is no evidence that any consequential rise in global mean temperature will have any harmful impacts on humanity. Indeed, the impacts might be beneficial.

5. If global warming does occur as a result of an increase of atmospheric GHGs, and if this warming does have harmful consequences, then action would be advisable. However, the George C. Marshall Institute estimated in 1992 that delaying action by five years could have a *maximum* impact of 0·1°C. To act now would be precipitate and costly.

The policies proposed are inefficient because:

1. A carbon tax would be unlikely to reduce CO_2 emissions significantly.[86]

---

85 See, for example, H.N. Pollack & D.S. Chapman, 'Underground Records of Climate Change', *Scientific American*, June 1993, pp. 16-22.

86 There are two reasons why this might be the case:

(1) Environmental taxes have historically been set rather low (see, for example, R. W. Hahn, 'Economic Instruments For Environmental Regulation: How the Patient Followed the Doctor's Orders', *Journal of*

[cont'd on p. 45]

2. Some economists have argued that environmental taxes have a 'double dividend'[87] on the grounds that they reduce both externalities and the distortionary effects of current revenue-raising taxes. But this is not true for a carbon tax: first, there is no proven externality, and second, largely because of the low price elasticity of demand for fossil fuels, the regressive 'welfare' effects of imposing taxes on coal, oil and gas are significantly worse than if the tax were levied on income or on other consumer goods.[88] So, rather than obtaining a double dividend, a carbon tax would actually have a negative dividend.

3. Since a carbon tax is unlikely to be introduced universally, any reductions in CO_2 emissions occurring in countries which do introduce a tax are likely to be at least partially offset by increases in countries which do not, as energy-intensive industries switch to these less-regulated areas. This, in turn, may jeopardize bilateral and multilateral trade agreements as pressure groups seek to restrict imports from 'offending' nations.

Economic Perspectives, Vol. 3, No. 2, Spring 1989, pp.95-114), acting more as revenue-raisers than as inhibitors. The carbon tax looks set to follow in this mould, with a high tax being politically sensitive, as the recent imposition of VAT on fuel in Britain (in two stages from April 1994) has shown.

(2) Fossil fuels are notoriously price inelastic (see, for example, D. Hawdon (ed.), *Energy Demand – Evidence and Expectations*, Guildford: University of Surrey Press, 1992) so, unless some cheap backstop technology comes on line, demand is unlikely to be much affected by a (relatively small) rise in price. One team of modellers has estimated that to achieve a 20% reduction in CO_2 emissions (relative to 1987 levels) would require a mean energy price rise of at least 421% (P. Caspros, P. Kasadelogou and G.N. Mentzas, *Carbon Tax Policy and its Impacts on CO_2 Emissions*, Dept. of Electrical Engineering, National Technical University of Athens, April 1990, p.12).

[87] See, for example, M. Pearson & S. Smith, *The European Carbon Tax: An Assessment of the European Commission's Proposals*, London: Institute for Fiscal Studies, December 1991.

[88] It has been estimated, for example, that reducing the US budget deficit by imposing a carbon tax would reduce GDP in 1998 by 0·2%, while reducing the deficit by raising income tax would reduce GDP by only 0·1%. ('Much Heat, Little Light', *The Economist*, 12 June 1993, p.35, citing R. Kopp of Resources for the Future.)

4. The argument against a European carbon tax is very strong: since Europe contributes only about 13 per cent of worldwide CO_2 emissions[89] (with the percentage declining as production shifts to developing countries) and its industries are already some of the most energy efficient in the world, any shift of production to less energy-efficient plants in other parts of the world may actually raise total global CO_2 emissions. Therefore not only would the people of Europe suffer but the tax would also be counter-productive.[90]

5. The current proposal for a European carbon/energy tax seems even less justifiable than a simple carbon tax. The only obvious environmental reason for such a tax would be the supposed externalities from non-fossil energy sources. However, these are as yet unquantified (and, we would argue, largely unquantifiable), and therefore the 50/50 split proposed seems arbitrary. Perhaps the reason why energy is included in this European tax is that the French obtain about 70% of their electricity from nuclear sources and would therefore have a competitive advantage were fossil fuels alone to be taxed.[91]

Subsidising Energy Efficiency Improvements

The arguments against such a policy are examined above (pp.39-40).

---

89 A. S. Manne and R. G. Richels, *op. cit.*

90 Some economists disagree: J. Pezzey (*Impacts of Greenhouse Gas Control Strategies on UK Competitiveness*, London: HMSO, 1993) suggests that a unilateral energy tax could raise the competitiveness (and overall welfare) of the society imposing the tax. But even in Pezzey's model this is only achievable if the country in question produces all the world's energy-intensive goods and has no indigenous fossil fuels. This hardly corresponds with the real world. Even if it did, one would imagine that production of such energy-intensive goods would soon shift to less expensive shores.

91 See also M. Pearson and S. Smith, *op. cit.*; F. L. Smith, *op. cit.*

Research into the Social and Economic Costs of Global Warming

It seems unwise to start (or, in many cases continue) subsidising research into the costs of a highly improbable eventuality. As we hope this Paper shows, it is not possible to estimate these costs. Until we understand the science better, social science research should wait.

Research into Climatology

While it would clearly be useful to have models with more predictive power, such models seem likely to be restricted by inadequate data for some years to come. In addition, it is likely that government funding would crowd-out private funding of research and would lead, as it has led up to the present, to the railroading of scientific research towards irrelevant models which attempt to put the 'blame' on man, rather than develop parsimonious models which try to account objectively for temperature changes.

Research into Geoengineering

Geoengineering means 'using brains not brawn'.[92] Attempting to reduce atmospheric GHG concentrations by limiting emissions is, Nordhaus suggests, the brawn method, while the brains method 'would introduce a hypothetical technology that provides costless mitigation of climate change'.[93] Examples might be: shooting mirrors into space to reflect sunlight, seeding the oceans with iron (which would fertilise the phytoplankton and algae, thereby increasing sequestration of CO_2),[94] or converting CO_2 from exhaust flues into useful chemicals.

---

92 W. D. Nordhaus (1991), *op. cit.*

93 W. D. Nordhaus (1992), *op. cit.*: but by 'costless' Nordhaus implies that the costs would be negligibly small.

94 A natural version of this may already be occurring. In addition to the sulphate aerosols released by Mt. Pinatubo, approximately five hundred million tonnes of iron were emitted. As, gradually, the iron has fallen back to earth (two-thirds of which is covered by water) there appears to have been an enormous

47 [cont'd on p. 48]

While climate change *per se* cannot be ruled out, it seems unlikely that the rate of change would be beyond the tolerances of the biosphere. Because adaptation is likely, geoengineering is unlikely to be warranted. Even if at some future time it appears that, for whatever reason, the earth's climate is changing at a rate faster than the biosphere is adapting, it seems probable that, in the absence of government subsidy, an enterprising individual or group will introduce an appropriate technology. Government funding would 'crowd-out' these entrepreneurs, thereby wasting taxpayers' money.

A 'What If?' Scenario

Before concluding, we would like to propose a totally non-scientific simulation of our own – a 'What If?' scenario.

When ice-age theory was in vogue in the mid-1970s, what if we had followed suggestions made then, by men such as Stephen Schneider (now a global warming proponent), and increased CO_2 emissions so as to increase radiation capture?

Subsidies to coal and other fossil energy sources would probably have been increased, as would taxation on income and expenditure to pay for these subsidies.

Both distortions would have slowed economic growth. The world would now be in a situation in which, if current global warming theory is to be believed, emissions of CO_2 would have to be cut by even more than is suggested today.

increase in algae blooms, resulting in the sequestration of about 1·6 billion tonnes of CO_2. (*Nature*, Vol. 365, 21 October 1993, pp. 697-98.)

Conclusion

Some special interest groups would gain from increased government intervention in the energy market. Such intervention would benefit some climatologists, energy and environmental economists, and environmental groups; the costs would be borne by consumers the world over. NASA's Dr Roy Spencer has observed:

'It's easier to get funding if you can show some evidence for impending climate disasters. In the late 1970s it was the coming ice age. Who knows what it will be ten years from now. Sure, science benefits from scary scenarios.'[95]

The story of this Paper is one of the manipulation of public finances to support 'believers' at the expense of sceptics, and to support hugely expensive public projects proposed by the Green lobby. Such railroading of investment and central planning of environmental and development goals is almost certain to be less efficient and less productive than private sector investment. Moreover, it may well, in time, prove counter-productive. In the words of F.A. Hayek:

'Is there a greater tragedy imaginable than that in our endeavour consciously to shape our future in accordance with high ideals, we should in fact unwittingly produce the very opposite of what we have been striving for?'[96]

There is a case for government withdrawal from actions which may be increasing GHG emissions – such as subsidising coal – but as regards further action we recommend governments do nothing.

---

95 Interview for 'The Greenhouse Conspiracy', Channel 4 Television, August 1990.

96 F. A. Hayek, *The Road To Serfdom* (1944), London: Routledge, new edition 1991, p.4.

Questions for Discussion

1. What is the so-called 'consensus view' of global warming?

2. How have scientific views on climate change altered since the 1970s?

3. (a) Does the empirical evidence support the consensus view? and

   (b) What are the key criticisms of the land-based data set?

4. Why do model forecasts give inaccurate predictions of today's temperature when run over the last century? What are the implications for forecasts of temperatures in 100 years' time?

5. What are the main problems with cost-benefit analysis?

6. How does uncertainty affect the way individuals make decisions? Should individuals adopt a different decision rule for dealing with uncertainty when confronting issues such as global warming?

7. How does government spending on scientific research and development affect private spending in this area?

8. How do taxes and subsidies on fuels affect the demand for these fuels? What would be the likely impact of imposing a Europe-wide carbon/energy tax?

9. Who are the prime beneficiaries of government action to combat 'global warming'?

10. How do market institutions react to environmental problems? If global warming was to occur, how might markets respond?

Glossary

CDIAC   Carbon Dioxide Information Analysis Centre at Oak Ridge, Tennessee.

CFCs   Chlorofluorocarbons. Hydrocarbon chains on which the hydrogen atoms have been replaced by Chlorine and Fluorine atoms. A class of greenhouse gases also implicated in ozone depletion.

CH_4 Methane. A greenhouse gas.

CO_2 Carbon Dioxide. A greenhouse gas.

EPA   Environmental Protection Agency. A US Federal body.

GCM   General Circulatory Model. A category of climate model, so called because they seek to model the full wind patterns of the planet.

GHGs   Green House Gases.

IPCC   Intergovernmental Panel on Climate Change.

N_2O Nitrous Oxide. A greenhouse gas.

NASA   National Aeronautical and Space Administration. A US Federal body.

ppm   Parts per million. A measure of concentration.

UKMO   United Kingdom Meteorological Office. The government agency involved in weather forecasting in the UK.

UNCED   United Nations Conference on Environment and Development.

UNFCCC   United Nations Framework Convention on Climate Change.

Further Reading

Publications marked with a ★ are available from the Institute of Economic Affairs.

★ Balling, R., *The Heated Debate: Greenhouse Predictions vs. Climate Reality*, San Francisco: Pacific Research Institute, 1992.

★ Beckerman, W., *Pricing for Pollution*, Hobart Paper No. 66, London: Institute of Economic Affairs, 1975, Second Edition, 1993.

Beckerman, W., 'Global Warming: A Sceptical Economic Assessment', in D. Helm (ed.), *Economic Policy Towards the Environment*, Oxford: Blackwell, 1991.

★ Bernstam, M., *The Wealth of Nations and the Environment*, Occasional Paper No. 85, London: Institute of Economic Affairs, 1991.

Boero, G., Clarke, R. & Winters, L.A., *The Macroeconomic Consequences of Controlling Greenhouse Gases: A Survey*, London: HMSO, 1991.

★ Cheung, S., *The Myth of Social Cost*, Hobart Paper 82, London: Institute of Economic Affairs, 1978, Third Impression 1992.

Friis-Christensen, E. & Lassen, L., 'Length of the Solar Cycle: An Indicator of Solar Activity Closely Associated with Climate', *Science*, Vol. 254, 1 November 1991, pp.698-700.

Fumento, M., *Science Under Siege*, New York: William Morrow, 1993.

Jastrow, R., *Global Warming Update*, Washington DC: George C. Marshall Institute, July 1992.

* Lal, D., *The Limits of International Co-operation*, Occasional Paper No. 83, London: Institute of Economic Affairs, 1990.

Lindzen, R.S., 'Global Warming: The Origin and Nature of Alleged Scientific Consensus', OPEC Seminar on the Environment, Vienna, 13-15 April 1992.

* Michaels, P., *Sound and Fury: The Science and Politics of Global Warming*, Washington DC: Cato Institute, 1992.

Nordhaus, W.D., 'To Slow or Not to Slow', *The Economist*, 7 July 1990.

Ray, D.L., *Trashing the Planet*, Washington DC: Regnery Gateway, 1992.

Ray, D.L., *Environmental Overkill*, Washington DC: Regnery Gateway, 1993.

* Robinson, C., *Energy Policy: Errors, Illusions and Market Realities*, IEA Occasional Paper No. 90, London: Institute of Economic Affairs, 1993.

Schelling, T.C., 'Some Economics of Global Warming', *American Economic Review*, January 1992.

Environment Books from the IEA

Free Market Environmentalism
Terry Anderson & Donald Leal, 192pp, 1991, £12.00 inc. P&P.

A statement of the theories that support the role of the market in the protection of the environment.

The Yellowstone Primer
John Baden & Donald Leal, 226pp, 1990, £12.00 inc P&P.

A collection of papers examining how free markets could better support the operation of this famous national park.

The Heated Debate
Robert Balling, 195pp, 1992, £12 inc. P&P.

Explodes the myth of global warming as unsupported by solid scientific evidence.

Pricing for Pollution
Wilfred Beckerman, 80pp, 1975, £5.45 inc. P&P.

Examines the economics of pricing and regulation and suggests ways in which regulation can be improved.

The Wealth of Nations and the Environment
Mikhail Bernstam, 71pp, 1991, £7.45 inc. P&P.

Looks at the relationship between wealth and environmental protection.

The Myth of Social Cost
Steven Cheung, 93pp, 1978, £6.45 inc. P&P.

A critique of the abuse of the concept of 'externality'.

The Limits of International Co-operation
Deepak Lal, 43pp, 1990, £4.50 inc. P&P.

A criticism of the theoretical basis of calls for international intervention, especially in the field of the environment.

Energy Policy: Errors, Illusions and Market Realities

by *Colin Robinson*

Colin Robinson – Professor of Economics at the University of Surrey, Editorial Director of the Institute of Economic Affairs, and the British Institute of Energy Economics' 'Energy Economist of the Year' – argues that British energy policies have been politically inspired, and are dominated by producer interests and short-termism.

Professor Robinson reviews British energy policy during the post-war years, showing how politicians were susceptible to arguments from energy producers that jobs (and votes) would be lost if they were not protected. The consumer voice was not heard – or, if heard, was not heeded.

The author attacks not only protectionist policies towards coal and nuclear power, but also the privatisation schemes for gas and electricity. The Government was not particularly interested in introducing competition into the gas and electricity markets. Its desire to raise revenue, and pressure from managements of the nationalised corporations, induced it to leave substantial market power in the hands of the privatised corporations.

The evidence suggests that 'government failure' is a much more serious problem than 'market failure'. If the aims are increasing efficiency, the best (though 'imperfect') answer is to rely primarily on energy markets.

Occasional Paper No. 90, ISBN: 0-255-36326-5, 62pp.,
£5.50 (including p&p)

Institute of Economic Affairs
2 Lord North Street, London SW1P 3LB.
Tel.: 071-799 3745
Fax: 071-799 2137

ECONOMIC AFFAIRS

the journal of the IEA

JUNE 1994

Deregulation Issue

The Market, Liberty and the Regulatory State — *Norman Barry*

Public Choice Issues in Social Regulation — *Martin Ricketts*

The Regulatory Crisis of the 1990s:
The Problem — *Christopher Booker*

The Regulatory Crisis of the 1990s:
Some Solutions — *Richard North*

The Government's Deregulation Initiative — *Neil Hamilton MP*

Regulation of Labour Markets in
the European Union — *Stan Siebert*

Beyond Regulation: An Analysis of Regulation
and the Alternatives — *Iain Smedley*

Government Regulation — The Way Forward — *John Blundell*

Regular Columnists

Sir Alan Walters, Jonathan Le Cocq, Tim Congdon, Roger Bate,
Geoffrey E. Wood

Plus

Letters and Comments

J. Parry Lewis, Keith Hudson, Lord Harris of High Cross,
Julian Morris, John F. Spellar MP

Book Reviews

Anna J. Schwartz, N. F. R. Crafts, Charles K. Rowley,
Geoffrey E. Wood, Allen Sykes

Published five times a year. Available on subscription
(Britain and Europe: £15.00 Institutions; £10.00 Individuals;
Individual issues £3.00 including postage and packing)

Institute of Economic Affairs,
2 Lord North Street, London SW1P 3LB
Telephone: 071-799 3745 Fax: 071-799 2137